CUSTOMS AND CULTURES OF THE WORLD

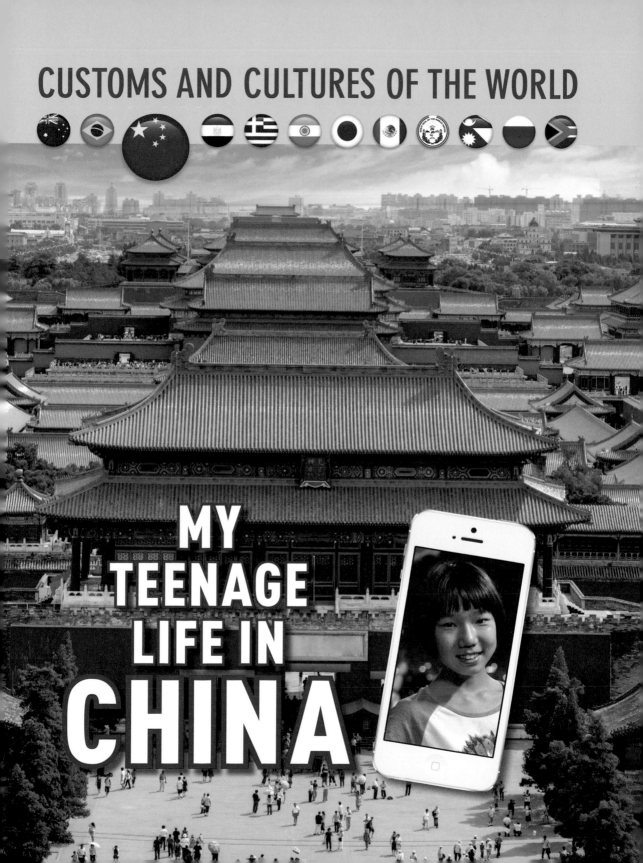

MY TEENAGE LIFE IN CHINA

CUSTOMS AND CULTURES OF THE WORLD

CUSTOMS AND CULTURES OF THE WORLD

Porter County Public Library

MY TEENAGE LIFE IN CHINA

By Jim Whiting
with Shi Yu Li

Series Foreword by
Kum-Kum Bhavnani

Mason Crest
450 Parkway Drive, Suite D
Broomall, PA 19008
www.masoncrest.com

First printing
9 8 7 6 5 4 3 2 1

Series ISBN: 978-1-4222-3899-8
ISBN: 978-1-4222-3902-5
ebook ISBN: 978-1-4222-7881-9

Library of Congress Cataloging-in-Publication Data
Names: Whiting, Jim, 1943- author. | Li, Shi Yu, author.
Title: My teenage life in China / by Jim Whiting, with Shi Yu Li ; series foreword by Kum-Kum Bhavnani.
Description: Broomall, PA : Mason Crest, 2018. | Series: Customs and cultures of the world | Includes index.
Identifiers: LCCN 2017003256| ISBN 9781422239025 (hardback) | ISBN 9781422278819 (ebook)
Subjects: LCSH: China--Social life and customs--Juvenile literature. | Teenagers--Social life and customs--China--Juvenile literature. | Li, Shi Yu--Juvenile literature. | Teenagers--China--Biography--Juvenile literature.
Classification: LCC DS779.43 .W55 2018 | DDC 305.2350951--dc23 LC record available at https://lccn.loc.gov/2017003256

Developed and Produced by Shoreline Publishing Group.
Editor: James Buckley, Jr.
Design: Tom Carling, Carling Design Inc.
Production: Sandy Gordon
www.shorelinepublishing.com

Front cover: Dreamstime.com/Hanhanpeggy.

QR Codes disclaimer:

CHINA

CONTENTS

Key Icons to Look For

Words to Understand: These words with their easy-to-understand definitions will increase the reader's understanding of the text, while building vocabulary skills.

Sidebars: This boxed material within the main text allows readers to build knowledge, gain insights, explore possibilities, and broaden their perspectives by weaving together additional information to provide realistic and holistic perspectives.

Educational Videos: Readers can view videos by scanning our QR codes, providing them with additional educational content to supplement the text. Examples include news coverage, moments in history, speeches, iconic sports moments, and much more!

Text-Dependent Questions: These questions send the reader back to the text for more careful attention to the evidence presented here.

Research Projects: Readers are pointed toward areas of further inquiry connected to each chapter. Suggestions are provided for projects that encourage deeper research and analysis.

Series Glossary of Key Terms: This back-of-the-book glossary contains terminology used throughout this series. Words found here increase the reader's ability to read and comprehend higher-level books and articles in this field.

SERIES FOREWORD

Culture: Parts = Whole

Culture makes us human.

Many of us think of culture as something that belongs to a person, a group, or even a country. We talk about the food of a region as being part of its culture (tacos, pupusas, tamales, and burritos all are part of our understanding of food from Mexico, and South and Central America).

We might also talk about the clothes as being important to culture (saris in India, kimonos in Japan, hijabs or *gallibayas* in Egypt, or beaded shirts in the Navajo Nation). Imagine trying to sum up "American" culture using just examples like these! Yet culture does not just belong to a person or even a country. It is not only about food and clothes or music and art, because those things by themselves cannot tell the whole story.

Culture is also about how we live our lives. It is about our lived experiences of our societies and of all the worlds we inhabit. And in this series—Customs and Cultures of the World—you will meet young people who will share their experiences of the cultures and worlds they inhabit.

How does a teenager growing up in South Africa make sense of the history of apartheid, the 1994 democratic elections, and of what is happening now? That is as integral to our world's culture as the ancient ruins in Greece, the pyramids of Egypt, the Great Wall of China, the Himalayas above Nepal, and the Amazon rain forests in Brazil.

But these examples are not enough. Greece is also known for its financial uncertainties, Egypt is known for the uprisings in Tahrir Square, China is known for its rapid development of megacities, Australia is known for its amazing animals, and Brazil is known for the Olympics and its football [soccer] team. And there are many more examples for each nation, region, and person, and some of these examples are featured in these books. The question is: How do you, growing up in a particular country, view your own culture? What do you think of as culture? What is your lived experience of it? How do you come to understand and engage with cultures that are not familiar to you? And, perhaps most importantly, why do you/we want to do this? And how does reading about and experiencing other cultures help you understand your own?

It is perhaps a cliché to say culture forms the central core of our humanity and our dignity. If that's true, how do young adults talk about your own cultures? How do you simultaneously understand how people apparently "different" from you live their lives, and engage with their cultures? One way is to read the stories in this series. The "authors" are just like you, even though they live in different places and in different cultures. We communicated with these young writers over the Internet, which has become the greatest gathering of cultures ever. The Internet is now central to the culture of almost everyone, with young people leading the way on how to use it to expand the horizons of all of us. From those of us born in earlier generations, thank you for opening that cultural avenue!

Let me finish by saying that culture allows us to open our minds, think about worlds different from the ones we live in, and to imagine how people very different from us live their lives. This series of books is just the start of the process, but a crucial start.

I hope you enjoy them.

—Kum-Kum Bhavnani
Professor of sociology and feminist and global studies at the University of California, Santa Barbara, and an award-winning international filmmaker.

MEET SHI YU LI!

李诗语

My Chinese name is Shi Yu Li; I am 15. Sheena is my English name, I use it when I talk to people who speak English. It doesn't have any legal meaning. You can call me my Chinese name. I am interested in history and current politics and also I like writing. I really want to share my stories and my opinions with you.

Editor's Note: This is a photo provided by our teen author. However, the other images of young women in this book do not depict her.

Subject: **My Family**

I must say that being underage in China, I'm pretty happy. There are two reasons. One is that the economy in China developed really fast for decades. My parents went through this period and they could feel that life was getting better every day. So for our generation, we don't need to worry about money or help our parents to make money. The other reason is that Chinese people see their children as the most important thing in their lives. In Chinese traditional culture, having no children is unkind to our parents and the elder generations. So children get the highest position in a family, especially when there is only one child [see page 26]. Our parents try their best to provide a better life for us and make sure that we get the best education. The parents in the cities are well educated and they know the importance of education. So as a Chinese child, I get a lot of attention and also a lot of preaching. Although while I'm growing up, parents seem pretty annoying and old-fashioned, yet I will never feel that I don't get enough love or feel snubbed.

I have lived in Beijing since I was born. My parents are from other provinces of China. They went to the university in Beijing and chose to live here for a better life. Now my family are all living in Beijing. Most of the time I stay in the city proper for school, but on vacations I usually travel to other places with my family.

I have been to America once and I really appreciate the education there. I really want to study there, but not until after I finish high school. I think family is also very important for a growing child so I want to stay around them.

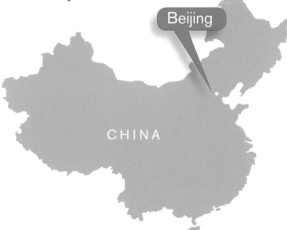

Beijing

CHINA

CHINA

China: An Introduction

Many people believe that the opening ceremonies of the 2008 Summer Olympic Games in Beijing, China, are the most spectacular that have ever been staged. Because the Chinese believe the number 8 is connected with prosperity and good fortune, the spectacle began precisely at 8:00 PM on the 8th of August (the 8th month) with the pulsating rhythms of 2008 *fou* drums. These are large, square, ornately decorated percussion instruments.

The organizers wanted to highlight the many accomplishments of one of the world's oldest and most important civilizations. Four of those accomplishments received special attention during the evening. Many people call them the Four Great Inventions because of their huge influence on the development of civilization around the world. They are gunpowder, the compass, paper, and the printing press. All originated in China and eventually spread around the globe.

Words to Understand

arable land   land suitable for cultivation and the growing of crops

dynasties   series of rulers connected by family ties

The organizers of the 2008 Summer Olympics in Beijing thrilled viewers around the world with a stadium-spanning spectacle in the Opening Ceremonies.

Another notable accomplishment featured during the course of the evening was the Great Wall of China. Nearly 900 performers made a miniature version of the wall, which is the longest construction project in world history. The first portions of the wall were built nearly 2,700 years ago. (A myth says that it can be seen from space. In fact, when Yang Liwei, China's first astronaut, returned to Earth in 2003, he said, "The scenery was very beautiful. But I didn't see the Great Wall.")

Land and People

Like those opening ceremonies, almost everything about China is on a massive scale. In area, it is the world's fourth-largest country, ranking just behind the United States. Fourteen countries border China as it sprawls across much of Asia. They are Russia, India, Mongolia, Kazakhstan, Kyrgyzstan, Tajikistan, North Korea, Pakistan, Myanmar (formerly Burma), Afghanistan, Vietnam, Laos, Nepal, and Bhutan. The Yellow Sea, East China Sea, and South China Sea form most of China's eastern border.

Because of its great size, China has a variety of natural terrain features. Mountain ranges occupy about a third of its total area and include the world's highest peak (Mount Everest). Deserts, wind-driven plateaus

The Yangtze River runs from west to east across central China. One of the longest rivers in the world, it plays a vital part in transportation, power, and irrigation.

at high altitudes, and vast forests account for immense swaths of territory where hardly anyone lives. By contrast, the lower-lying landscape in the east and south contains most of the population and the **arable land** that sustains it.

China also boasts two of the six longest rivers in the world. One is the Yangtze, which stretches for nearly 4,000 miles (6,437 km) and ranks behind only the Nile and the Amazon in terms of length. The other is the Yellow River, which at 3,395 miles (5,463 km) long ranks sixth.

Today, the country has the world's largest population. It may also be the most diverse. The government officially recognizes 56 ethnic groups. By far the largest is the Han, who account for about 92 percent of China's population. Counting the Han populations of Taiwan, Malaysia, Singapore, and other countries, the group accounts for nearly 20 percent of the world's entire population.

Admiral Zheng He

Starting in the early 1400s, Chinese officials sent seven different fleets of hundreds of ships each throughout the Indian Ocean and the South China Sea to establish their control of the area and open up trading relationships. Admiral Zheng He commanded the fleets. His largest ships were nearly 400 feet (121 m) long, 150 feet (45.7 m) wide, and had up to nine masts. They were the largest wooden vessels ever constructed. Christopher Columbus' three ships would easily have fit onto their decks, with plenty of leftover room. Zheng He wasn't even Chinese. He was born in Central Asia, far from the sea. He was captured and taken to the Chinese emperor's court, where he established himself as a powerful leader and, eventually, a world-ranging sailor.

China's Dynasties

While Chinese history dates back thousands of years, most people date its history by the names of the ruling **dynasties**. The first was the Xia, which began more than 4,000 years ago. In most cases, though, the rulers of the earlier dynasties controlled only part of the country.

Perhaps the most important ruler was Qin Shi Huangdi. He ruthlessly united numerous warring factions in 221 BCE and became the country's first emperor. He introduced a standard system of weights and measures, linked several segments of walls into the Great Wall, and suppressed any criticism of his rule. It's likely that the name China came from him. Qin is pronounced as "chin." Despite his accomplishments, though, the dynasty he founded was the shortest-lived in Chinese history.

Soon afterward, a series of trade routes began developing in China. These routes became known as the Silk Road after the first major product to be traded along its length. Eventually it reached the West and created a

This medieval manuscript shows travelers moving along the Silk Road, the vital trading route that connected Europe to China and other parts of Asia.

The Mongol conqueror Genghis Khan once ruled over a territory stretching from the Caspian Sea in the east to the China Sea in the west.

demand for Chinese goods. Material goods weren't the only commodities that traversed the Silk Road. Buddhism was introduced into China by this means. Today nearly 20 percent of the Chinese population are Buddhists. That is nearly half of the worldwide population of Buddhists.

One of the most famous dynasties was the Yuan. It was founded by Genghis Khan, who swept out of Mongolia to seize northern China. His grandson, Kublai Khan, conquered the rest of China. Marco Polo traveled to Kublai Khan's court in 1275 and wrote a book about his experiences in the country. It became a bestseller in Europe and made people there much more aware of the wonders of China.

No person had more effect on China since the days of the Khans than military and political leader Mao Zedong, who established the current government of China.

To the Present Day

The last dynasty was the Qing. During the early part of the 19th century, Great Britain imported large quantities of Chinese goods, especially tea, silk, and porcelain. But the Chinese had no interest in British merchandise, which created a trade imbalance. To solve that "problem," the British began selling the drug opium to China. The money they "earned" this way helped offset their purchase of Chinese products.

Many Chinese became addicted to the powerful drug. The government objected. The British used its military might in two Opium Wars to force China to allow the opium trade to continue and open up the country to British goods on terms unfavorable to China. Those defeats reduced Qing control of the country. Other countries such as France, Germany,

Japan, and the United States also forced China to sign trade agreements that benefited them and harmed China even further. A brief but bloody conflict in 1899 known as the Boxer War tried to kill the foreigners living in China. All the occupying countries sent their troops, and the uprising was quickly suppressed.

The last Qing emperor was Pu Yi. He ascended to the throne in 1908 at the age of two. Four years later he was overthrown and China became a republic. Two main factions began fighting for power. One was the Nationalists, led first by Dr. Sun Yat-sen and then Chiang Kai-shek. The other was the Communists, under the leadership of Mao Zedong. The two factions formed an uneasy alliance during the Japanese occupation in World War II. After the end of the war in 1945, they resumed their struggle. The communists defeated Chiang's forces in 1949. They made People's Republic of China the official name. China remains a Communist country today. ✷

20th century China

SHI YU LI'S SCHOOL LIFE

To: **The Reader**

Subject: **My School**

Most of the teenagers in China go to state schools as I do. I'm a student in grade three, class 11. The full name of our school is the high school Affiliated to Renmin University of China. It's the best school in China and all my classmates and teachers are proud of being part of it! There are two parts of a high school. One is the junior high and the other one is the upper high school. Each school has three grades. The two schools usually have the same president and use the same resources such as classrooms, library, gyms, and labs. Also, they share the same name.

When we finish junior high school, all the graduates in Beijing will take a unified exam that includes math, physics, chemistry, Chinese, English, history, geography, biology, and sports. The marks you get will decide whether you can go to a good high school. And of course, a better high school means a bigger chance for a good university. Taking this exam is the only way to get into a good state high school. My teachers and I will try our best to prepare for the exam in the coming year. You can feel yourself under a high expectation and a big pressure. But it's inspiring to see that your classmates are all working hard, too. All the teaching, homework, and tests we have in the three years is for having a better grade in this especially important exam. It's pretty superficial but there are no other ways to get a better education besides having a better mark. Each grade in our school has 15–20 classes, and each class has 40 students. So that's a lot of people. The classmates and the teachers who teach us hardly ever change in the three years. So we have a very deep friendship.

To: The Reader

Subject: My Subjects and Activities

Beside the subjects I have mentioned, we have politics, swimming, dancing, music, art, technology, and psychology. What's more, we have selective courses. We can choose cooking, economics, astronomy, acting... whatever we want. There is even a class to teach you how to start your own company! Some classes are taught by someone who is very professional such as a professor from a college and others are maybe just a group of students. There are more than 100 such classes and it's easy to find the one you like. It's very interesting and meaningful, we can make friends who have the same interests with us and know more about the things out of the school. All in all, I am pretty satisfied with my school and my school life now. I am happy to see that I'm wiser and stronger everyday.

SHI YU LI'S SCHOOL LIFE

MATH ROCKS!

My favorite subject is math. Thinking logically is exciting and challenging. I really enjoy the process of finding the key points, chasing the clue, opening my mind, coming up with ideas and trying different methods until I finally get the correct answer. Also, I think doing math problems can make me more sharp and wise. It helps me to solve other problems, too.

To: The Reader

Subject: My Next Move

When I go to college, I want to study physics or philosophy. I am still trying to figure out what I want to do, and sometimes I have a lot of confusion. I can't wait to figure out how this world works and what's the true meaning of life. I don't think college education can help me work out all these problems but I think it's a good beginning of this adventure of a lifetime. The biggest goals in my life are to write an encyclopedia with all my experiences and opinions in. It doesn't matter whether someone else will read it or like it, I just want it to be a reality writing of my life and the world I live in.

TiME TO EAT!

THREE CUPS CHICKEN

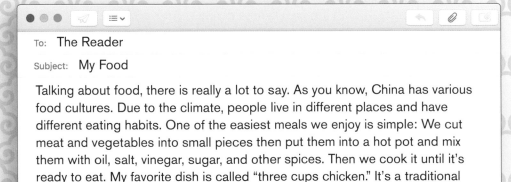

To: The Reader

Subject: My Food

Talking about food, there is really a lot to say. As you know, China has various food cultures. Due to the climate, people live in different places and have different eating habits. One of the easiest meals we enjoy is simple: We cut meat and vegetables into small pieces then put them into a hot pot and mix them with oil, salt, vinegar, sugar, and other spices. Then we cook it until it's ready to eat. My favorite dish is called "three cups chicken." It's a traditional food from Taiwan. I can't make it well so I usually have it in restaurants.

To: The Reader

Subject: My Breakfast

For breakfast I usually have a bowl of cereal with milk. I need to leave home for school at about seven, and my parents go to work even earlier. They always have breakfast at the cafeterias at their offices. So for me, it's a good choice to have a quick and easy breakfast. I have lunch at school with my friends. We eat some rice and hot dishes. My parents cook dinner when they go back home. I sometimes lend a hand. The dinner is similar to lunch. My parents and I sit at the table talking about how our day was while eating. It's a relaxing time of day.

CHINA

TIME TO EAT!

To: The Reader

Subject: Different Foods I Like

In a city like Beijing, it's easy to try food from other countries. I like Japanese food, Korean food, and American food. They are delicious but I still think Chinese food is the best in the world. Going to restaurants is prevalent in China. We like restaurants as much as people in Western countries like bars and coffee shops. Talking about coffee shops, we actually drink a lot of coffee, too, especially among students and young employees who often stay up late for work.

Shi Yu Li
Squash Pancake
Like • Comment • Share

I am willing to try new food and I am definitely a food lover. But I don't like to make it. The most important reason is that cooking Chinese food needs to use heat and it's easy to make a lot of smoke. And I'm kind of afraid to do that! The only food I'm able to cook well is squash pancake.

First, you braise the squash and grind it.

Then mix it with some flour and water.

Then put the smooth paste into a pan and shape it into a cute circle! My grandma taught me how to make it—she is really good at cooking.

Chinese Culture

One of the most important elements of Chinese culture is a tight-knit family structure. It's common for three generations—parents, children, and grandparents—to share the same home. The Chinese also **venerate** their ancestors. This family structure is one of the legacies of the noted Chinese philosopher Confucius, who lived about 2,500 years ago.

For many years, Chinese families were large. This was due to high levels of infant mortality—that is, you needed to have more babies to make sure you had enough of them survive—and the necessity for as many people as possible to work in the fields. In the years after the communists took control, large families threatened to exceed the ability of the country to produce enough food. In 1979, the government announced the One-Child Policy to slow population growth. Families with more than a single child had to pay a fine. Though the policy began to be phased out in 2015, families often still have only one or two children due to the expense. Especially in rural areas, many parents prefer to have boys so the youngsters can help in the fields.

Words to Understand

mausoleum   a large building used as a burial site

terra cotta   brownish-red fired clay

venerate   treat with great respect

Many of the stories told in Chinese opera and drama are from the early history of the nation and include elaborate traditional costumes.

Art

China has one of the oldest traditions of art in the world. Chinese opera, one of the country's most popular art forms, combines singing and music with martial arts, acrobatics, and other vigorous movements.

Poetry and other forms of writing date back thousands of years. Most Chinese painters reflect the beauty and serenity of nature rather than doing portraits and often include brief inscriptions in a corner of the image. These inscriptions reflect the importance of calligraphy, the art of beautiful penmanship with a brush, to the Chinese.

Sculptures dot the Chinese landscape. The most famous example of Chinese sculpture is the "underground army," which was discovered

in 1974 near the **mausoleum** of the first emperor, Qin Shi Huangdi. It consists of a pit filled with thousands of life-size **terra cotta** soldiers marching in battle order. Additional pits contain cavalrymen and other troops. Incredibly, each figure has its own distinctive face and hairdo and may have been modeled on real soldiers.

CONFUCIUS

Confucius was born in 551 BCE, during the Warring States period, when the country was splintered into many small kingdoms. After working as an administrator in one of those kingdoms, Confucius spent most of the rest of his life as a wandering teacher. Because of the chaos and violence of the Warring States period, Confucius valued order and stability. He believed in obedience to authority. One of his main lessons was that everyone in society had a particular role to fulfill and should be content with that role. Subjects should respect their rulers, and children should respect their parents. It was also important for rulers to rule wisely and justly and treat their subjects fairly. And everyone needed to remain in control of their emotions and be kind to one another.

Medicine

Another important part of Chinese culture is a long tradition of medicine. It is based on the concept of *qi*, the Chinese word for energy and the life force. *Qi*, in turn, is divided into two halves: *yin* and *yang*. *Yin* stands for what is called the female principle: Earth, darkness, and passivity. *Yang* is the male principle, with such characteristics as light and activity. For many years, Chinese physicians believed that the two principles needed to be in harmony for optimum health. The symbol for good health is a circle composed of what resembles two interlocking single quote marks—one black and the other one white—with each one including a dot of the opposite color.

On a more practical level, Chinese medicine was often far ahead of the West. Chinese physicians recognized that blood circulates through the body, vaccinated people against smallpox, and performed surgery centuries earlier than their counterparts in the West. They have a long tradition of herbal remedies.

China works with animal conservation groups around the world to expand the population and health of the famous pandas.

And many people are familiar with acupuncture, in which needles are inserted into the patient's skin to help the flow of *qi*.

Any discussion of Chinese culture must include the giant panda and the dragon. The dragon historically has been China's national symbol. In recent years, pandas have taken on at least part of that role. Few animals are as immediately recognizable with their fuzzy black-and-white fur and black patches around their eyes and ears. Sadly, pandas are an endangered species. According to estimates, no more than 3,000 are in the wild, with fewer than 300 in zoos.

Sports

Many martial arts originated in China. Actor Bruce Lee helped popularize martial arts in the West during the 1970s through films such as *Enter the Dragon*, *The Way of the Dragon*, and *Fist of Fury*. A decade later, actor Jackie Chan achieved worldwide fame through a combination of breathtaking stunts and frequent flashes of humor.

A martial art called tai chi was originally used for self-defense. Now it has become a form of gentle exercise to calm the body and reduce stress. It's not uncommon to see hundreds or even thousands of people at a single location practicing tai chi.

Chinese athletes do well in international competition. They won 121 gold medals in Summer Olympics from 2008–16, more than any other country. Since badminton was introduced into the Olympics in 1992, Chinese players have won 18 gold medals. That is two more than the total of all other nations combined. Diving began in the Olympics in 1904, but China didn't compete in the sport for 80 years. Nevertheless, it is second in overall medal standings with 69 (the U.S. leads with 138). In recent years, Chinese divers have been especially dominant, winning 10 of a possible 24 medals in 2016 (including seven of eight gold). Weightlifting is another strong Olympic sport. The Chinese have 57 total medals, second only to the Soviet Union/Russia. Swimming, gymnastics, and shooting are other international sports in which Chinese excel.

Ping Pong

Table tennis (more popularly known as ping pong) became an Olympic sport in 1988. Since then China has won 53 of a total of 100 medals, including 28 of 32 gold. Their dominance resulted in a rules change in 2012. Each nation could only enter two players. That prevented the Chinese from taking all three medals.

At the 2016 Summer Olympics in Rio de Janeiro, Chinese athletes won as many table tennis medals as every other country combined, including all four golds.

Table tennis also extends beyond sports. In 1971, the U.S. and China were enemies. The Chinese invited a team of U.S. table tennis players to China for a series of matches. Many people believe that the resulting tour produced a thaw in U.S.-Chinese relations and paved the way for President Richard Nixon to open diplomatic relations with China. As a result, the tour is often referred to as "ping-pong diplomacy." ✳

Chinese table tennis

SHI YU LI'S TOWN

To: **The Reader**

Subject: **My Town**

Beijing is a magnificent city with a long history and also a modern style. I love it and I see it as my hometown. Beijing is not built in blocks and it's quite sad to see walls everywhere. But when you get used to it, you can find that it's a friendly city. I like it because in a city like Beijing you can also find some surprises, such as an old shop hiding in the end of a small road. I don't know much about the Chinese traditional culture, but I enjoy walking in the old buildings, admiring how exquisite they are and wondering what stories had happened in there. What's more, Beijing is a modern city and it's developing really fast. It's a good place for young people who are looking for opportunities and like to try new things.

The communities in Beijing are all very crowded as the house prices are pretty high. We live in tall apartment buildings, which usually have 20 floors or even more. The relationships between neighbors are usually not close. We don't even know what jobs they do or where they are from. As the people in the neighborhood are not that close and friendly, we don't have any community activities or works. It's quite sad to see that people who live together are unconcerned with each other.

Street Food

National Museum

I think the normal tourist spots are already enough for you to understand the Chinese culture and history. And they truly are the best part of Beijing. If you want to see more about this city, you can spend more time at the museums, such as the National Museum of China or the National Museum of Art. I think museums about science in Beijing are not so good as Western countries, it's better not to spend time at these places. What's more, try new food by eating the traditional Chinese food. Going to the places which local people like to go is always a good way to enjoy your trip!

Silk Market

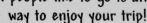

My advice on visiting Beijing is to take subways and use the Google map. The subway is cheap and easy.

 CHINA

Chinese Customs

China is especially noted for its many festivals and celebrations. Many date back hundreds or even thousands of years. Here are some of the most important.

Two New Years

Like people throughout the world, the Chinese celebrate January 1 as the New Year. They also celebrate the Chinese New Year, which is based on the **lunar calendar**. It occurs on a different date every year, on the new moon between January 21 and February 20. It is the most important cultural and civic holiday in China. It is so important that many countries with large Chinese populations celebrate it as well.

Words to Understand

cadence   beating time to establish a regular rhythm

equinox   the date twice a year when the sun crosses the equator, making the day and the night of equal length

lunar calendar   A calendar based on the period from one moon to the next. Each cycle is 28 1/2 to 29 days, so the lunar year is about 354 days

saltpeter   A chemical compound that combines potassium, nitrogen, and oxygen and is used for fertilizer and medicine in addition to explosives

City centers around China are heavily decorated with traditional red lanterns to celebrate the New Year's events, usually in February.

Each year in the Chinese calendar is centered on one of 12 animals. So 2017 is the year of the Rooster, while 2018 is the Year of the Dog. The other animals are (in chronological order) Pig, Rat, Ox, Tiger, Rabbit, Dragon, Snake, Horse, Goat, and Monkey. Children stay up late on Chinese New Year's Eve in the belief that it helps them to live longer. Chinese make sure their houses are completely clean to get rid of all the *huiqi*, or inauspicious breaths, which have accumulated during the previous year. They often wear new clothes.

According to an ancient tradition, an evil monster called the *Nian* attacked villages. The monster had a particular appetite for children. Eventually the people discovered that the *Nian* feared bright lights, loud noises, and the color red. So Chinese New Year's festivities are always

well lit. People continually set off firecrackers. The dominant color is red, in banners, decorations, flowers, face painting, and much more. Children receive money—in red envelopes.

The Lantern Festival occurs 15 days later, at the peak of the full moon. People decorate their homes and streets with lanterns made of tough, waxy paper with a candle or other light source inside. They also eat *Tangyuan*, balls made with rice flour and water. The balls are bright and shiny, just like the moon.

Tomb-Sweeping Day

Reflecting the importance that the Chinese place on the family and showing respect to their ancestors, they celebrate the Qingming Festival on either

Families gather in April for Tomb-Sweeping Day, visiting the graves of their ancestors to leave flowers and offerings, and to honor the departed.

April 4 or 5 (the 15th day after the Spring **Equinox**). It is also known as Tomb-Sweeping Day. The festival dates back to the 700s. Wealthy individuals frequently honored their ancestors with elaborate and expensive ceremonies. Tang Dynasty Emperor Xuanzong decreed that such ceremonies could only occur once during the year.

Today, people visit the burial sites of their ancestors during the Qingming, cleaning them up and offering brightly colored flowers and small amounts of food. They also wear willow branches or place them on the doors of their houses, in the belief that those branches ward off evil spirits that may be active during the holiday.

In addition to showing reverence, the day serves as an opportunity to have fun because winter is over and spring has just begun. So families enjoy spring blossoms, sing and dance, and fly animal-shaped kites. When night falls, they attach lanterns to the tails of the kites to make them seem like twinkling stars. They round

The Big Bang

New Year's and other Chinese festivals make good use of fireworks. Fireworks are one common use of gunpowder, one of China's Four Great Inventions. Around 850, Chinese scientists were experimenting with compounds using **saltpeter**. They wanted something that would prolong life, maybe even create immortality. Some of them tried mixing saltpeter with sulfur and charcoal. To their surprise, "smoke and flames result, so that [the scientists'] hands and faces have been burnt, and even the whole house where they were working burned down," according to an eyewitness account. While gunpowder was quickly adapted for military purposes, its entertainment value was also obvious. Technicians pour gunpowder into tubes, then add chemicals and small pellets. The result: "oohs" and "aahs" as the gunpowder explodes in midair, creating a spectacular variety of colors and shapes.

In dragon boat racing, teams of paddlers in decorated craft stream along rivers and lakes. An onboard drummer helps them keep pace.

out the festival by eating traditional foods such as sweet green rice balls and crispy Qingming cakes.

Honoring a Poet

Qu Yuan was a famous Chinese poet who committed suicide by jumping into a river about 2,300 years ago because he was unhappy with the corruption in the emperor's court. The nearby villagers went out in boats to search for him, but they were too late to save him. So they threw rice into the water to feed his spirit. During this era, people believed that dragon gods lived in rivers and were responsible for rain, which was necessary for the growth of rice. They made offerings to the dragon gods.

Today the Dragon Boat Festival usually occurs in early-to-mid June, depending on the lunar calendar. The centerpiece is a dragon boat race, which may be derived from the boats that searched for Qu Yuan. Dragon boats are long, narrow craft with up to 40 paddlers on each side. An elaborately carved dragon's head is at the bow and a tail is at the stern. A leader controls the boat with a rudder and bangs on a drum to establish the **cadence** for his oarsmen. Dragon boat racing is so popular that many communities stage races, and there is even a world championship.

National Day

Another important holiday is National Day, which falls on October 1. It marks the anniversary of the official founding of the People's Republic of China in 1949. That ceremony took place in Tian'anmen Square. With 300,000 people packing the square, Mao Zedong raised the new nation's flag.

The always-crowded Tian'anmen Square in central Beijing becomes even more packed when people gather to celebrate National Day on October 1.

Today the flag is symbolically raised again, with an honor guard accompanying it. The celebrations help remind Chinese of how far they have come since the humiliations of the Opium War era and subsequent foreign domination. Like the Fourth of July in the United States, many shopping malls offer significant discounts on merchandise, people line the sidewalks to watch patriotic parades, and revelers shoot off fireworks.

National Day is also the first day of Golden Week, during which Chinese workers have a full week to themselves. Many take the opportunity of the long holiday to visit relatives in distant locations, tour the country's many attractions, or simply relax and enjoy the time off.

American children are always jealous to hear about the annual Children's Day in China, which honors the young and features performances, parades, and parties.

Common Holidays

The Chinese have several celebrations in common with many countries throughout the world. Starting in 1950, China joined in celebrating National Women's Day on March 8. Chinese women enjoy a half-day holiday, and their husbands and children do special things for them. Four days later the Chinese celebrate Arbor Day, which is celebrated around the globe depending on climate and the growing season. Everyone between the ages of 11 and 60 is asked to plant at least one or two trees and may be subject to fines if they don't. China chose March 12 to honor the death date in 1925 of Dr. Sun Yat-sen, one of the founders of the Chinese Republic in 1912.

National Day celebration

Like many other countries, the Chinese celebrate May 1 as International Labor Day. The day honors the contributions of workers to the well-being of Chinese society. (It is interesting that International Labor Day originated in the United States—which of course celebrates its workers on the first Monday of September.) And they also honor the nation's young people on Children's Day, which is celebrated on a wide variety of dates worldwide. One of the first acts of the new People's Republic of China was choosing June 1 as the date. Youngsters aged 14 and younger get to stay home from school. ✳

SHI YU LI'S FREE TIME

I don't mind going to places alone. I even went to the Tian'anmen Square at late night one day by myself just to see the picture of Mao. (That's not a political action! I just went there to have fun as it is the only place which is still open at that time except the bars. And hanging in the city alone is a pretty cool thing for us.)

To: The Reader

Subject: My Free Time

On long vacations I usually travel to other places in China or other countries. And in the short holidays I like to go out with my friends who are also my classmates. Sometimes we go to the museums and galleries or some tourist spots such as the Summer Palace (right) and the Temple of Heaven. Other times we go to the malls to watch movies and shop. We usually go out by subway or taxi. My parents won't bother me on this! I am able to go out and have fun anytime I want if I finished my work. I really like hanging out.

Shi Yu Li

My Free Time

Like • Comment • Share

Sometimes I like to stay at home listening to music and reading books. I like to read classic novels like Tolstoy's works and some science fiction like Hunger Games. My parents like history and art. And I sometimes read the books that they suggested I read.

Most of the teenagers I know like listening to music. We have different styles and like different things. I like the English songs and I hardly ever listen to the Chinese songs or Japanese songs, which are also popular. My favorite singers are Lana Del Rey and Lorde (below). I listen to songs on Billboard every day. I don't have a lot of money to buy albums so I usually use some music apps on my phone.

CHINA

SHI YU LI'S FREE TIME

I hardly ever watch TV, but sometimes I watch soccer games. My favorite team is Atlético Madrid [a pro team from Spain; in red].

In China, we have TV programs similar to America's. We have cooking shows, reality shows, documentaries, and TV series. The biggest difference is that our news shows are all under the control of the party, that is, the Communist party of China. But our news now is quite objective and not as emotional as it used to be. I am really interested in how media in other countries report the news. I'd like to know their opinions on some global events.

Subject: **Helping Out**

Being a member of our school volunteer group is the best thing in my school life. We are the guides in the museums. We go to the orphanage to take care of the kids. We gather books in our school and send them to the poor students in other places. We help other student groups and teachers to hold meetings and activities, too. It's so great to see that your actions can really bring others advantages and happiness. It also taught me how to communicate with strangers and give others what they actually need. I improved myself through this.

CHINA

Chinese Economy and Politics

Just over a century ago, China was still relatively backward in terms of economic development. Agriculture was the primary economic driving force. In recent years, the country has seen explosive growth in industries such as mining and manufacturing. China now has the world's largest workforce and the highest value of industrial output. Many products, especially electronics, are made in China because workers are often paid much less than in countries such as the United States. In some cases their working conditions are poor, such as 12-hour work days, six days a week, and exposure to harmful substances. However, media pressure and new policies can lead to improved workplaces. Wages in general are rising,

Words to Understand

cash crops   crops grown for direct sale in a market

parliamentary   referring to the legislative, or lawmaking, branch of a government

viable   capable of surviving and continuing to function

warlords   military commanders who control a particular area of a country, especially when the central government is weak

With more than a billion people to feed, China has an extensive agricultural section of its economy. A big emphasis is on rice, wheat, and similar grains.

and increasing numbers of people have more money to spend—often on the very things they are making.

About half of all Chinese workers are still employed in agriculture. China is the world leader in the gross value of its agricultural output, especially rice and wheat. Other important crops include apples, barley, corn, millet, peanuts, potatoes, sorghum, soybeans, and sweet potatoes. In terms of **cash crops**, China ranks first in the world in cotton, tea, and silk.

Toys Are Us

China is by far the largest toy manufacturer in the world, producing about 70 percent of the world's playthings. The boom in toymaking shows no signs of diminishing. In addition to vast amounts of exports, the increasing prosperity of Chinese themselves means more domestic consumption, as people want their children to have fun. The majority of Chinese toy companies are small to medium-sized, though some supply directly to major US companies such as Mattel and Hasbro.

Tourism is another important industry. For several decades after the communist takeover, the country discouraged tourists and carefully monitored the few foreigners who did enter the country. In recent years, interest in China has surged and it is currently the fourth-most visited country in the world, behind France, the United States, and Spain. Some experts believe that in 2020 it will be the most popular tourist destination. Because of the relatively easy access, South Korea sends the most people to China—more than four and a half million every year.

Tourists from Beijing throng to the amazing Great Wall of China.

The Long March

China's road to economic dominance has not been smooth. The Republican government established in 1912 lasted just a few years. After that the country descended into chaos, with a variety of **warlords** controlling different areas. Life was difficult for peasants, who often had one warlord replace another—usually by violence. In 1926, Chiang Kai-shek led an army against the warlords and defeated them with the aid of the newly formed Chinese Communist Party.

Then he turned against the communists. After several years, Chiang seemed on the verge of victory. His troops had encircled most of the remaining communists, but they broke out and fled to safety in a 6,000-mile trek called the Long March (1934–35). Although many died during the year-long retreat, enough survived to keep the party

Mao Zedong drove Nationalists out of China to establish the Communist state.

viable. The Long March also established Mao Zedong firmly as the leader—he had been a librarian when he joined the Chinese Communist Party.

During World War II, the communists learned valuable guerrilla fighting tactics as they fought the Japanese occupiers. They also dealt kindly with the peasants, in what was known as the "hearts and minds" policy. When the war ended in 1945, communist forces became increasingly successful against Chiang's army and emerged victorious early in 1949. Chiang and his followers retreated to the island of Taiwan to form the Republic of China.

After Mao

At first, things went well under the communist government, which controlled all the land and the means of production in the country. China had little contact with the rest of the world. But starting in 1958, what was called the Great Leap Forward became a giant step backward. Several harvests failed and millions of people starved to death. Then in 1966 the Great Proletarian Cultural Revolution tried to re-establish what Mao thought were the revolutionary ideals that resulted in the victory over Chiang. In the resulting chaos, the economy suffered and created hardships for many people. In addition, more than a million people were killed and millions more were imprisoned or humiliated. China's education system suffered because many teachers were accused of the "wrong" kind of instruction. One result was what is often called the "lost generation," millions of poorly educated youngsters lacking basic knowledge and skills.

Xi Jinping became China's president and general secretary in 2013.

Mao died in 1976 and his successor, Deng Xiaoping, halted the revolution and condemned it for its excesses. He also opened up the economy, especially encouraging foreign investment. The benefits were almost immediate. Farmers were given more control over the land they cultivated. He also allowed factory managers to determine the appropriate production levels rather than dictating them from above. That put China on the road to economic growth rates of up to 10% every year. Deng's successors have maintained a similar approach.

One-Party Government

However, China still remains a one-party government—the Chinese Communist Party. Though the National Peoples Congress has nearly 3,000 members—making it the largest **parliamentary** body in the world—it has little real power. Many people regard it as a rubber stamp for decisions made at the highest levels of the government.

The government often cracks down on people who object to its policies. The most famous incident came in May 1989. As many as a million protestors packed the streets of the capital city of Beijing and its vast Tian'anmen Square. On June 4, Chinese soldiers supported by tanks cleared the demonstrators by force. According to government figures, 200–300 protestors and soldiers died. Unofficial estimates put the figure at up to several thousand. Many people maintain that human rights abuses in China continue to this day. *

"Tank Man"

The day after helping to clear Tian'anmen Square, the tanks began rumbling away. A lone man, dressed in white shirt and black pants and holding a shopping bag, stood in front of one of the columns of tanks trying to leave. The lead tank tried to maneuver around him. The man shifted his position to block the tank. Then he climbed onto it and talked with the crew. Eventually two men pulled him away from the vehicle and into the crowd. No one knows the man's identity or what happened to him. But photos and videos of "Tank Man's" defiance created a sensation. In 1998, *Time* magazine included him in its feature "Time 100: The Most Important People of the Century."

SHI YU LI'S COUNTRY

ESSAY: MY COUNTRY

Shi Yu Li

I think that although our country has many problems like air pollution, a growing gap between rich and poor, and diplomatic issues, I still live a pretty good life. I like China because it is a free country. Tradition and modern are well connected here. You can do things as your personal style and no one will judge you (well, that is true just for teens . . . when we go to work, we have to do things as our boss wants, just like our parents do).

My Fellow Citizens

The citizens may be dissatisfied with the government, but they probably just say it to people around them to make them feel that they have thoughts. But they do nothing. That's what I don't like about China. I think it's okay for a country to have problems. But if the citizens just complain about it and never do something real, these problems may never be solved. There are even a lot of people who spread their emotional opinion on the Internet and make people feel that they live in a terrible country! I can't understand that; if they want to be heroes who can make the country better, why don't they do so? Their statements just make the disunity even more serious.

Chinese Leadership

I know that some people in other countries are unhappy about what China does. I want to say to them that if you are not happy about what the Chinese leadership did on some global issues, I have nothing to say. You probably know that Chinese people have little rights on the national things; we can't decide what our leadership did. I believed that every leadership in different countries are trying  to defend the rights of the people they represent in a legal way and not to make the people in other countries get hurt at the same time. No one wants a war. Through World War One and Two, we can see that there is no final winner in a war. Peace is the only way to provide everyone on this earth a better life and a better future. Now, eight countries already have nuclear weapons and more than 44 more are going to have one [eventually]. With so many bombs, we can easily turn this whole world into a wasteland. So I don't think that any nation will be so stupid to hurt other nations and having a World War Three! Some politicians say that China is evil and wants to have a war. I think the purpose of this statement is just to earn more supporters in their countries. So I think we can both relax and be nice to each other.

The Environment

I am also worried about the environment in our country. The economy grew so fast that no one wants it to stop it, although the factories, cars, garbage, and pollution clearly damaged the environment. I think we will

SHI YU LI'S COUNTRY

pay a price for this in the future. I hope I can still live in Beijing in the future. I have had so many sweet memories here and I don't want to leave here for anywhere else. But if the air problems can't be solved in time, I will have to leave here for my health.

Outside the City

I think teens around me are all pretty happy and satisfied. But not every teen in China is as lucky as we are. A large number of teens in countryside are lonely as their parents left home for working in big plants in cities and hardly ever come back. They have to take care of their younger sisters and brothers and their old grandparents who still live in the countryside. And at the same time they need to make money for their poor family. They don't have time to study but education is the only way to step in a higher class. So when they grow up they can only do some simple work in factories and get a low salary like their parents do. And when they have children, it will probably be the same.

> Only a few people in China have faith. We don't care about it so much. The power of faith in China is so weak that it can neither decide [politics] nor social morals. No one will judge you for having no faith. You just respect others' faith, then it's okay.

Faith in China

Religion is a sticky subject in China. Officially, the Chinese Communist Party is athiest, though national laws say that people are free to worship as they choose. The government recognizes only five faith traditions: Buddhism, Catholicism, Taoism, Islam, and Protestantism. Further, it uses national power to try to control some of the institutions of those faiths, such as appointing its own Catholic bishops or choosing its own Dalai Lama for Tibetan Buddhism. Some "minor" faiths are persecuted, too. However, studies show that the number of Chinese participating in some form of religion—even ancient folk-based practices—has risen steadily since the early 1970s.

The Future of China

As the Chinese look to the future, people around the world watch to see what they will do. That's because its future is perhaps the most important element in global stability. China is still undergoing many changes as it moves forward.

One of the biggest questions about China's future revolves around the economy. For years the economy consistently experienced one of the highest annual growth rates in the world. Can this growth rate continue? Some analysts say it can, provided that the government takes steps to make more markets open to private-sector competition. Others say the government fears a loss of power if it does that and therefore won't take the necessary steps, in which case the economy may become **stagnant**.

Words to Understand

indigenous   living things native to a particular area

stagnant   unmoving, staying in one position

It doesn't look like much, but this reef and coastline on one of the remote Spratly Islands might be the flash point of a major international incident.

South China Sea

China's status as one of the world's great military and economic powers means that whatever the government does outside its borders will have major implications. One example is the South China Sea. China's newly found economic muscle helps make the region the most heavily trafficked sea route in the world. In addition, it's likely that the seabed of the South China Sea contains immense reserves of natural gas and oil.

China has established what it calls the "Nine-Dash Line," which encircles nearly all of the South China Sea and all the land it encompasses as well as the seabed and its potential riches. This line not only creates tensions with other countries that border on the sea but also the United States, which has pledged to defend those countries if need be. China

enjoys one huge strategic advantage: It is in essence the "home team," whereas the U.S. must send ships and aircraft thousands of miles for any possible engagement with Chinese forces. And it would be impossible to send ground troops in any significant numbers.

One of the key potential flash points in the South China Sea are the Spratly Islands. The Spratlys have no **indigenous** inhabitants and consist of a number of tiny islets and reefs that add up to about three-fourths of a square mile of land (490 acres, much smaller than New York City's Central Park) spread over a sea area the size of Montana. The Spratlys are important for several reasons: They contain rich fishing grounds, may have significant reserves of oil and natural gas, and lay astride heavily traveled shipping lanes.

Because of the Spratlys' strategic location, four countries within 200 miles (322 km) of the islands—Brunei, the Philippines, Malaysia, and Vietnam—all claim them. Though they lie nearly 500 miles (804 km) away from its mainland, the Chinese also claim them and are building artificial islands and putting military bases on them. While conflict with the other four countries is a possibility, the mostly likely confrontation is with the U.S. because American warships sometimes sail through the Spratlys to enforce the idea of freedom of the seas.

Three Gorges Dam

The Three Gorges Dam is China's largest engineering project since the construction of the Great Wall and is the largest power station in the world. Chinese officials hope the dam will provide up to 10% of the country's energy needs, prevent catastrophic flooding, and provide water for farming from the 400-mile lake it created, while also preventing the burning of 30 million tons of coal each year. On the other hand, more than a million people lost their homes to the rising waters behind the dam, many important archaeology sites disappeared beneath the lake—which is becoming increasingly polluted—and blocking the river has negative effects on wildlife, especially fish and marine mammals.

Bad Air

China is the world leader in both energy consumption and air pollution. The rise in industrialization in China has led to serious air pollution in some of the major cities, especially Beijing, Hong Kong, and Shanghai. One of the primary causes is burning coal for the power to run all the machines. That increases asthma and coughing in people from tiny particles contained in coal smoke that enter the lungs. People often wear gauze masks in an attempt to screen out those particles.

One of the main challenges facing the government in the coming years is to cut down on this pollution. The country has high hopes for the Three Gorges Dam on the Yangtze River. It is the world's largest hydroelectric dam, but has created its own environmental concerns. And more and more people are moving to already overcrowded cities, where inhabitants consume up to four times as much energy as rural dwellers. Clearly, China has its work cut out for itself as it strives for cleaner air.

Place in the World

Perhaps the biggest issue facing China, however, is its place in the world. For decades, it has clearly been one of the major world powers. With a new administration taking over in the United States in 2017, many experts wondered what effect that will have on relations with China. When running for office, Donald Trump had a lot of tough talk about what he thought about China. Once in office, what will he do about relations between the countries? Will they remain the same, or will they change? For China and the world, this is a story to watch carefully. ✳

TEXT-DEPENDENT QUESTIONS

1. What are the Four Great Inventions?

2. In what sports is China most successful in international competition?

3. What was the Long March and why was it so important in Chinese history?

4. What happens during the Qing Ming Festival?

5. Why are the Spratly Islands so important?

RESEARCH PROJECTS

Look into these topics:

1. Describe Qin Shi Huangdu came to power, and why his dynasty didn't last long after his death.

2. Write a short essay about the long history of the Great Wall, and its effectiveness in keeping enemies out of China (or not).

3. Explain how the Opium Wars harmed China and created resentment against foreigners.

4. How did the Boxer Rebellion get its name, and what actually happened?

5. Research and discuss the strange and curious history of Pu Yi, China's last emperor.

FIND OUT MORE

Books

Cotterell, Arthur. *Ancient China*. New York: DK, 2005.

Flower, Kathy. *Culture Smart: China*. London, UK: Kuperard, 2010.

Morton, W. Scott and Charlton M. Lewis. *China: Its History and Culture*. New York: McGraw-Hill, 2005.

Ropp, Paul S. *China in World History*. New York: Oxford University Press, 2010.

Websites

www.timeforkids.com/destination/china
Time magazine's introduction to China for young people. It includes a, timeline, sightseeing guide, and a day in the life of a 12-year-old Chinese boy

www.cia.gov/library/publications/the-world-factbook/geos/ch.html
Country overview with brief descriptions of China's geography, government, economy, people, and more.

afe.easia.columbia.edu/special/china_1750_opium.htm
An explanation of the causes and consequences of the Opium Wars. It includes discussion questions.

SERIES GLOSSARY OF KEY TERMS

arable land   land suitable for cultivation and the growing of crops

commodity   a raw material that has value and is regularly bought and sold

cuisine   cooking that is characteristic of a particular country, region, or restaurant

destabilize   damage, disrupt, undermine

dynasties   long periods of time during which one extended family rules a place

industrialization   the process in which an economy is transformed from mainly agricultural to one based on manufacturing goods

infrastructure   buildings, roads, services, and other things that are necessary for a society to function

lunar calendar   a calendar based on the period from one moon to the next. Each cycle is 28 1/2 to 29 days, so the lunar year is about 354 days

parliamentary   describes a government in which a body of cabinet ministers is chosen from the legislature and act as advisers to the chief of state (or prime minister)

resonate   echo and reverberate; stay current through time

sovereignty   having supreme power and authority

venerate   treat with great respect

INDEX

Photo Credits

Alamy Stock: Everett Collection 49. AP Images: Jeff Widener 51. Dreamstime.com: Indos82 9, Etherled 11, Xianghong Wu 12, Henge01 15, Tom Wang 18, Racom 20, Martinmark 21t, Mohamed Osama 21b, Beijing Hetuchuangyi Images Co. Ltd 22, msphotographic 23t, Radist 24t, Hurry 24b, Ivanna Grigorova 25, Spaxia 25, Inna Chernish 25, Kelvint 27, Hupeng 29, grosremy 31, Miao 32, Rafael Ben-Ari 33bl, Hou Guima 33tr, Radist 33tl, Eagleflying 35, Hupeng 36, Lee Snider 37, Guanglian Huo 38, Eastimages 39, Janbinglee 40, Qin0377 42t, Icara 42b, Turkburg 43t, MaxiSports 44t, humphery 45l, Raywoo 47, Wxmh 48, Enrique Calvoal 50, Wing Ho Tsang 52, Jbron 53, HSC 54, Xianghong Wu 54, Maocheng 55. Shutterstock: Lee Snider 44b, Chameleons Eye 45r. Wikimedia: Kurt Stauffer 43b, Matthew/LyangLyang.

Author Bio

Jim Whiting has published more than 180 nonfiction books for young readers. He is the most prolific childrens' author in his home state of Washington. His subjects literally run the gamut from A(ntarctica) to Z(ionism). His goal is to write a stack of books taller than he is. Right now the level is at his collarbone. (Thanks to Cameron Reid and Bei Li for their helping in connecting with Sheena and her family in China.)